HOOF

HOOF

Kerrin P. Sharpe

TE HERENGA WAKA
UNIVERSITY PRESS

Te Herenga Waka University Press
Victoria University of Wellington
PO Box 600 Wellington
teherengawakapress.co.nz

ISBN 9781776921225

A catalogue record is available from
the National Library of New Zealand.

Written with the support of a grant from

Printed by Blue Star, Wellington

for my husband, Gordon Davidson

Contents

/

hoof

The train with the chest
of a horse and the traction
of old intelligence

turns from the power stations
and cooling towers
and heads for the trees.

Through his mane of rain
and nostril smoke
float poems of blocked arteries,
quadruple bypasses.

Sometimes he finds a good line,
goes somewhere –
sometimes all he brings his brothers
and cousins is the stutter
of drinking songs.

In a new forest he finds
the sockets of branches,
the tongues and roots of stumps,
the whoosh of leaves.

He finds logs in the lake
sap on the round house,
the turbine the turbine –
rooks, crows, industrial corn

now add to the gloom
of his siding room
where he writes all night
in search of light.

the blackbird mistakes

The blackbird mistakes
my blank page for snow,
his wings shadow my pencil.

My hand becomes a beak,
my spine hollow bones
and feathers of a blackbird's hump.

He peck-pecks the paper
like rain, sleet, hail –

I write *tree*
        he's in the branches
I write *house*
        he's on the roof
I write *garden*
        he's found a worm.

Now the poem's
a blackbird's watch tower,
a waiting room so cold

his gizzard rattles
the oldest song
it should be snowing . . .

When I write *sky*
as quick as a full stop
he's back in the world

his eyes white blades
on the horizon.

flint

To live in a forest
in the grounds of a palace,

to watch thousands of blackbirds
become one bird,

to find them one morning
on the forest floor,

to think they must be
plums in snow,

to forget the guns
on display, on call,

on the wall at the palace,
to remember

you believed
that first staccato cracking

was a traveller with a flint axe
harnessing sparks to boil water.

I've never written to please Ted

An elm pushed by the wind
falls like scaffolding around the church,

the trunk wide as a crow's yawn,

as the boy's yawn, the boy who smokes,
saws a branch, smokes, saws a branch,

takes a break, stares at the trunk
where it fell, where it stays,

where gracious bells
scatter darkness from Percy's pale coffin

carried over the trunk
where two fox cubs now live.

still

Trees are leaving
the canopies they built,
the crowns they fashioned,
the music they made.

Trees are leaving –
claws clamped,
growls muzzled,
pelts barbed,
snouts bound with chains,

their dance cut short,
their dance felled.

Trees are leaving
with fur in their hearts
and honey in their blood,
the divinity of the forest
still inside them.

just like heaven

The horse is in a hammock
held by steel wheels and hooks.

Ropes share the force and distance
of his fractured cannon bone.

The horse with no medical history
has such faith in the surgeon

that the anaesthetist
can hardly breathe himself.

The sick and the dying
stroke the horse, they walk

in his hooves, they climb
back in their saddles.

more horse than castle

Blinkers of rain, cliffs of mist,
shoulders of hillocks.

We drive under capes of pines
past Constance's wedding dress

and *Cornus controversa*,
the wedding-cake tree,

past the ballroom where Kate was laid out –
weeping broom, Chatham Island forget-me-not –

and around the Alice Lawn to the lodge,
once a hoofie house

where horses shopped for shoes,
their cart now a bed in room 27.

In the loft a fake horse
models Lanarch's tack.

It's alarmed –
by what?

You can't fool a horse

the weight of moonlight

The moon rides a horse
to open the pelt of sky.
It's not unusual for the horse

to be overcome by the moonlight
or for the moon to have phases
of carrying the horse.

*

Brides of the moon
rise from rivers,
empty their shoes,

clatter onto open-deck buses,
throw and catch their own bouquets,
smile for one photographer.

*

I watch Benedict Cumberbatch
orbit the London Eye
his near side facing me.

We hold moonlight like water.
I wonder, do I catch my bus here
or *here*? No, *there*, he points.

*

In the queen's stables, rings of horses
dream of leaving the moon.
The ravens cry
Too soon! Too soon!

a retired pilot flies asleep

his pockets fill with mountains
and bad weather

everything's falling

sons
daughters
landing gear

home he shouts
to remember the word

his house is off-site
off where?

he'll never fit back on earth

St Kilda pray for him
St Clair pray for him

there's no one gluten-free
there's no one
where's the sea?

he ditches the plane
he blinks awake

the trumpet player

You cannot recall
trumpet lessons, only the glow
of your father's cigarette
and follow-up cough.
And you remember the darkness
of the concert halls.

Though the mine had long stolen
most of your father's breath,
he still loved to hear
your lungs flare like wings.

One reviewer likened your playing
to Gustav Mahler conducting a wind farm.
Predictions tonight are for gales
in exposed places.

South of the divide,
with trumpet in one hand
and suitcase in the other,

you accompany the wild totem
of the wind.

sure-footed

When she started school, everyone ran to the mat
at show-and-tell time. You had to *wait* your turn.
You had to be *chosen*. Even then
she wished they would get on with it. Even then
she knew being half of anything was difficult.
Though she flew round Redcliffs like pīwakawaka
she knew when Jonathan, her twin, was hurt.
She does not remember how she changed a girl called Joan
into a Karitane nurse. She does remember
how she found perspective in the arms of the walnut tree
in Duncan Street. While she sleeps in Reserve Terrace,
high cranes from the port weave a path.
She never stumbles over broken wooden boats.
Sure-footed. Meaning, her small soft leather boots.

on a night angry enough

The shadows of Hokitika tussle with the sea.
They fall, rise, slide to shore,

drift like wood, whistle like bone,
whirr like green, dance like stone.

Some limp to the memorial clock tower
and find their names.

Some rattle the smoko window
of the old milk factory.

Others – their backs bent like harakeke –
wrestle rain to reach the Hokitika River,

and prise open muddy seams of consecrated water
to release those miners

drowned on boats
in the terrible rush,

drowned with dreams of gold
in the rage of a bridgeless river –

now their faces are rock
now their faces are ice.

The shadows weave a northern path
of rough, layered schist,

opening the mouth of the river
returning their breath to the sea.

half-mast

Leonardo, the oldest
of the fishing fleet, blessed
with holy water, good weather,
the sea's bounty, grace –

Leonardo, a scapula
of half-mast Italian flags,
still hearing the sea swallow
Vincenzo/Gennaro/Paolo/Ronaldo –

Leonardo, circling like a wreath
where they disappeared,
begged back by priests
with candles, with lanterns –

Leonardo, overwhelmed in Rita's painting
Boats' Island Bay, on postage stamps
and posters, *Leonardo* half-hearted –

half his mast now finials
on the roof of a boatshed,
guiding like wooden stars
the mothers of wanderers here below.

the park

At cricket practice
he whacks the ball higher than ever

wows his team

then collapses   not kidding
not breathing

his Labrador a circle   of worry
the leaves   in an uproar

sirens   sirens   sirens

Early next morning, the park
is a quiet place

we cross
        because we can

sister

She skates to Reverend Mother's funeral.
The lake is frozen, the nun's fingers
are frozen on the same Hail Mary.

Her hair waves like corn.
Later her hair falls like ash
from her burnt scalp.

She carries her hair to court
in a plastic bag.

Soon she's radioactive.
Her throat grows thorns,
or scar tissue, or tries to close.

On the lake she grows
as light as her hair.

who?

Sick of field fairies burning his turf wall,
Dad built one around himself.

In his old passport he has a halo of curls.
It was the sixties
and whenever footage of the Irish Troubles
came on, he left the room.

Rumours from his village followed him
across the Pacific –
    shot in the leg kicking a ball
    hidden in barns attics chimneys
    an incident at a railway station . . .

Perhaps that was why he needed elbow room,
    to fish in a river all night,
    to pray in an empty church,
    to stare at the sky.

After his stroke, all his words jumped ship
except for *who?*
He went from a man who read dictionaries
like novels to a man fluttering between worlds,

and after the funeral a stranger rang to say
Dad had been on his watch list.

instead angels

minded my mother,
spinning heat from four tall candles.
A ring of angels never worn thin,
turning bowing angels
threading blessings through her hair,
kneeling, never leaving, and I
hurried home to tell her this
then remembered she was still
in the locked chapel, in the flickering
light. How I wish I'd stayed the night.

in loco parentis

The turbines keep an eye
on my parents.

They chant around their grave
like monks in a friary,

the air so sacred
I never worry

about leaving them
in a cemetery.

In spring, the turbines
disperse airborne spores,

and a moss who never even
knew my parents

shields their headstone
with its green arms.

Even now, though, whenever
there is a strong wind warning

I cannot help praying
the turbines will yield

the energy to renew
my parents to bring them back home.

because they are buried in another city

My parents don't expect visitors
so strip down to their bones
in soil so lumpy
it feels wrong to stand on.

From the cemetery, my son sends
photos of their flower-holder
plugged with forget-me-nots,

and their headstone, both names:
loving wife and mother

loving husband and . . .
'father' the only word
silenced by moss.

My son is soon to be a father.
Is this a code for

1   my father's joy at the news
2   my father's claim he'd never heard the news
3   the baby's first word?

if you're looking for Leonard

Today he's expected at Tower Hill Station.
The train arrives, like a poem,
with snow from Berlin and leaves from Manhattan

and (in a darker version)
twigs from the Feng trees of Shanghai on its roof.

Once Leonard appears, the platform becomes
both a place by the river and a table of mercy.

He doesn't make them angels, he doesn't
make them lonely – songs they sing together
songs they never know.

If you're looking for Leonard,
just mention his name,

he's holding the flame
for the Passover train.

sometimes she walks

Sometimes she walks a path lined with feng trees,
walks a canary in a tiered bamboo cage,
walks a cat on a leash; I see the Great Wall,
all those steps leaving one life for another.

Egrets and orioles watch her cross the Plum Bridge,
wave to the ferryman, gather herbs beside a stone path,
rescue insects stirred up by donkeys' hooves.

Through the fog, the temple bells.
There's honey in the air. My daughter makes food wraps
out of wax and decorates them with the calligraphy of bees.

She paints chopsticks with wolf hair brushes,
fingerpaints tiny poems: *pale moon snowy mountains*
goldfish. Signs her new name, 迪迪

Her head is shaved, her head is covered in corn sheaves,
her head is bowed, she wears a loose jacket and trousers
plainly woven from long-fibre cotton with a 300-thread count
as she teaches the long slow movements of Tai Chi.

In a teahouse she pours congou, oolong, souchong.
On Sundays she visits the grave of her new father.
Back home her old father still faces the sea, turns 70,
stents, diabetes, glaucoma, arterial vascular disease,
he never gets used to it.

Last night I dreamed she was at the Terracotta Hospital,
repairing a warrior horse. The horse
waited to stand. I dreamed the legs
were in pieces, no two hooves the same.

Kalene Hill 1948: the baby won't turn

Nurse McGregor fills the cylinder
with nitrous oxide and oxygen,

and the mother soon forgets
the spotted hyena will find

the roast she hid in the tree.
Nurse McGregor knows about

malpresentation, and the breech baby's legs
extend like an antelope's

when she manipulates the two blunt blades
of the obstetrical forceps.

Outside, a hooded cobra
crosses the red earth road

and the baby's father cycles faster
towards the brick Mission Station.

en route to Fish Hoek

Our father checked the radiator
and forgot all about the hand brake,
but we never forgot being left inside
the green Austin at the top of the hill,

or how our father chased the rolling car
and left his Panama hat in the air,

and because not one of us could reach the handbrake,
we learnt that day about gravity and physics.

We never forgot how the Bedford truck
lumbered out of the dust at the bottom of the hill
and positioned itself for impact,

or how, when our father reached us and we all knelt
in the red earth, how our baby began to feed.

ballet

There are photographs of Rose
dancing on the shores of the Mediterranean
and in Lebanon,

photographs of her dancing
on narrow paths between buildings in Palestine,

photographs of her carrying rice and good water
through community kitchens to queues of refugees.

There are photographs of Needham
raising his great-great-grandfather's
waka from a swamp
and heading north to Auckland,

and photographs of his arrival
at the anchoring place,
the *Mea Culpa*, photographs of him
eating hoki with Rose.

The sun grows softer.
The air lifts their feet.

can you help us William Blake?

He is stranded above the new shoreline.
The heavenly music of the sea
                              a dream.
The merry rocking cradle of the sea
                              a dream.

Walls of water fall like Jerusalem
so water divides water
                              into water,
and any visions Blake draws
                              travel rapidly

and vanish at a single point
into the temple of waves,
                              then angels
rise from the ocean – some of them
                              parched,

some of them confused by the strange
currents and wind patterns – and hand
                              Blake the reins.

sculpture

Two whale flukes
lit at night
escape their stone world,
pretend they live
                    somewhere else.
Leap like islands,
sing deep slow songs –
where are
                    their babies?
Early morning they're
back on the plinth,
breathless salty-dry,
so warm they wake
                    all of us.

the sea takes a wife

a poem in two voices

he builds a bach at Boulder Bay
on rock and crusty sand
holds his winter wedding there
the speeches, the banter
his baby's to be induced
his wife's worry as heavy as water
lighter when she swims
the baby rocks her uterine bed
through her mother's skin
her thin thin voice
I'm not ready   yet
the woman lifts her shoulders
her arms like oars
a long desperate prayer
for forgiveness
the woman and baby
will never be closer
the woman swimming
the baby turning like a waterwheel

the sea drowns the coastline
singles out the bach
admires the sloped roof
watches the window
the bach becomes anxious
doesn't sleep, doesn't eat
grows small, burrows deep
tries to hide
the sea undercuts foundations
wave cuts weatherboards
takes the upper hand
there's crayfish on the table
a fire in the grate
from macrocarpa
the man plants a surf break
the sea with lips and arms
warming the rising water
carries the surf break
like a bride

cliff top wedding

The bride is first to notice
the little blue penguin.

Her words are wind-eaten
before they even reach the sand:
w   h   r   s
y   r   m   t   h   r?

The penguin gives a hoarse bark
as a southerly whooshes through the open-air marquee,
pinning guests to plastic chairs . . .

Even from the beach, the penguin can smell
dressed salmon, king prawns, crabs,
can hear them blown straight from
platters to the rocky floor.

The penguin's stomach is empty –
so many fish it never caught
and chased too long into nets of cooler water.
The sea booms. The swell

rises, veils the penguin
with foam and spray,
carries it home.

hoopla

six lemon tulips from the bride's bouquet
stand on tippy-toes in a deep glass vase,
drink with guests in the seaside living room,
become flushed, lean north, doze on their stems.
Someone in a rabbit skirt has so much to say.
I've known him longer than any other woman . . .
The microphone passes out, the sea wrestles bottles
and cans, it's the shortest day, only the tulips notice
the swell. Open the front door – there's surf everywhere.
The bride tries to rescue the tulips.
Her ring swims round and round on her finger.

the ways of rain

The open grave of the window cleaner.
His coffin apple-bobbing the sides.
His wreath of roses, their polystyrene boat.
The mourners, unsure whether to look.
The priest: *He leads me beside the still waters.*
The mourners, unsure whether to smile.
The mourners, remembering the words
of the window cleaner: *I've one eye*
against the sky. The window cleaner, forgiven
for overlooking the ways of rain,
forgiven for all those dirty dinners
he fed the sea. The ways of rain, deep,
deep as a saviour's love, giving
the window cleaner a way to row home.

wai anake | only water

A mother floats, swaddled,
in an egg-shaped tank.
       She drifts in slow circles,

nudges the walls
like a mime artist –
       her baby when ready

fizzes like a starfish,
ignores the raised voices
       of blades, of hooks,

rows through labour,
waves not even the sea
       can hold.

The minutes rise like tides.

The waves break,
The waves swell.
       The curl of fish voices,

the coil of baby,
the waxy blood moons,
       spume / shingle / stone.

                    *

from wai anake / with love

to the baby who grew in water
thriving in the deep parts
       the hush of grace

who heard rain before
it became a word
    who remembers standing

on sea and river beds
and not drowning, who remembers
    the warm arms of water

he moana pukepuke
e ekengia
    e te waka

a choppy sea
can be
    navigated

*

Wai anake / only water,
guardian of the baby,
    day after day, tender.

Tells stories, plays
rough-and-tumble music,
    winds the baby down,

tucks the baby in
every night
    like an island.

Teaches the baby
to read water, body roll,
    shoulder lift, front crawl.

Teaches the baby
to gather logs swept downstream
    in heavy rain,

to lash things together
with flax,
    to fashion

from forest debris
a floating chapel
    where the baby,

an apostle of water,
lights votive candles,
    the baby

with so much reverence
for water
    we're forgiven.

think

braided by sunlight
sea-ice glacial-ice
like hair in currents that
deliver the latest in plastic
to marine life
think all occasions
think all sizes snug slimming
fishing nets the mainstay *yes*
of any wardrobe *look* cotton
buds hands-free options for
seahorses *look* nose-straws
guaranteed to stay put
in larger nostrils *plus* full-length
non-breathable plastic capes
suitable for storm and other birds
plus bottle caps suitable for tiny
houses *think* rock pools *think*
clean me

testament

1
a wedding party arrives
at the Cavendish
the wind lifts
blue moon rose petals
off a bride fragrant
with light blessed
at the synagogue
testament to the Book
of Proverbs the Book
of Jeremiah
below the pier
a labrador already
frantic for the bride's bouquet
churns the mucky surf

2
a ghost train pinches
the jewelled octopus
swings her tin carts high
over the pier
fuses helter-skelter lights
side-kicks barrels of music
locks the jaws of clowns
spits at mechanical hares
jams the rifle range
the sea's persistent cough
shoots thick phlegm
into the jittery waves
six silver turbines
up to their necks in it

3
in the honeycomb of the pier
the homeless raise their voices
to fidgety angels
strung along the promenade
the light fades
Christmas drifts to sea
large parts not suitable
for over-threes
pincers of plastic
claws of sticky oil
all those logs from where?
seagulls tumble
just as helpless
as the coastline

sinew & snow

The medical train cracks the ice
of a small Russian settlement
not on any map.

It's -60° between the mountains.
The wind sings in a baritone
to traumatised pines
and cottages wear great coats of snow.

The villagers find their teeth,
open their doors, milk their goats,
bake red-cabbage pies
and meet the train with lunch.

They don't want to see doctors,
they want to be with them.

Like Lazarus the doctors
unwrap their patients,
and the light wakes bedsores,
back pain, blood pressure.
Watch the drink, put spittle
on your warts, lock up damp rooms.

Then everyone crosses
the frozen rough creek
to the cemetery.

While the oldest babushka
reads the names of the dead,
the younger men light birch torches
and sprinkle vodka
over the graves, then all link arms.

never

I hope the Nenets
never leave this poem,

never dread the deep freeze
that follows warm rain,

never see reindeer
stamp and click their hooves,
never worry the moss and lichen,

never grow weak,
starve
lie down
and never walk again,

never watch heat waves
melt the permafrost,
release anthrax,
poison reindeer,
a small boy,

never help the herd
cross fields of roads,
force them under rafters
                    of pipes,
force them under the arms and legs
                    of pipes,

never hear the gas flare's
hungry song
                    at Bovanenkovo.

it could be colder

Those clouds are polar bears
seeded with gold
from the sun.
In utero as long as
it takes.
Wonderfully made bears
at high, soft windows.

instead of travelling north

The storm is so strong the windsock lies down.
Polar bears huddle in broken houses.
One of their cubs chews a phone charger,
one cuts his lip on a mayonnaise jar.
Sometimes, in the way of bears,
they see-saw on planks and barrels
or roll and chase perished tyres.
Nothing sounds like ice.
Through fog the bears point seawards.

a road falling away

what if you had a grandfather
you'd never met who lived
on the Arctic tundra

what if he was woken
by hundreds of trees
moving in lines towards his hut

what if those trees
smothered the lichen and moss
that he fed to wild deer

what if he saw
a rare white reindeer
running through the birches
and thought of you

what if he decided to use
the last days of ice
to carve you a deer

what if he carried that deer
through ankle-high puddles
where once he'd captained ships

and knocked at your door
with nothing of the deer
nothing in his arms

when you greeted him

blue

Your blue wooden house
still nestles in Niaqornat,
        Johanna.

The washing line, once
a bunting of towels and nappies,
        stands empty,
the breathy songs of narwhals
dried by the wind.

Last night in the front room,
Johanna, four tall candles
        held stillness
around you, an orchestra
of faith in light,

and when morning arrived
with the sledge you were blessed
        with herbs and moss,
the whole village behind you
all the way to Chapel.

Do you remember saying
the ice would never change?
        These days
it's too thick for boats,
too thin for sledges.

Some hunters shoot their dogs.
Unmended nets lie on the beach.
        What happened
to elbow grease, Johanna?

Everyone's on the internet,

there's not a kayak
            in sight.
Lately, a low grey sky
hangs over Niaqornat.

So many stay indoors,
forgetting
            who they are.
Waves nibble away the cliffs.
What if the ice left

and never returned,
what then, Johanna?

from letters to Johanna

Circles of light on your wedding ring,
your fingers clenched *just* and unclenched *push*.
The midwife fluttered between the kitchen table
and kettle. Hunters in Niaqornat lay on the tuvaq,
listening for a whale.

*

Once, I dreamt oil from the *Exxon Valdez*
crept all the way from Alaska into Niaqornat.
We ran down to the stony beach, tripping over
towels and blankets, sea birds, sea otters, seals,
cormorants in their thick shrouds, eyes open,
eyes closed, eyes missing, Johanna, you, the first
and longest in the water, day after day, tenderly wiping
and wrapping the dead, the injured, in words
from anchor songs.

*

I've never forgotten Olayuk climbing the rise home,
calling snow geese, telling us he'd married in a chapel
powered by ice, telling us he'd woken the next morning
singing to himself, Olayuk pushing back his caribou hood
and stamping back towards the sea, shouting,
No one will remember me!

*

The little snow girl your Alfred built the last time
he ever walked – how her arms opened wider every day.
How, like him, she faded into ice and smoke.
Prayers of the morning, prayers of the evening.
His thin bruised hands.

*

Cries of pink-footed geese made smooth with leaving
still float around Niaqornat, cries that suspend you,
Johanna, between waking and sleeping, today your
house perched on tongues of slippery wood seems
jittery, maybe it hears the rage of carbon and methane,
these days the melt is so much earlier we've hardly time
to hunt or store meat like we did, it's been ages since I've
heard a whale, last month the air was warmer than bone.

map ice show

Antarctica – a bold footprint
on a picture atlas,
so magnetic nothing moves.
The huts like nests.
The scientific research
is close-lipped.
Deep marine life fears no ill,
ice is trapped in sculptures,
never to rise or drown.

*

Under the ice, creatures
grow nets, gorge themselves,
speed date brittle stars,
abandon eggs
for televised births,
fill their blood
with anti-freeze and other tricks,
spin through the ocean
on hooves, stilts, scooters
of lime tendrils,
bribe larvae to grow
spinal cords the length
of rulers.

*

Antarctica plays continuously
as the simulated wind chill
reaches -18°. Sirens count down
the arrival of extreme weather.
Tourists take frantic selfies
in their polar outfits
then run in terror from the storm.

the imitation of ice

Whenever the music box plays,
three children skate on a pond. It's dusk,
so it's dinner time and the houses
are lit. The doors don't open, so no one
calls their child to dinner.
Houses stay lit because of the music.
Children skate because of the music.
Parents never call their children to dinner.
Children never return to their houses.

The brittle plaster pond stays warm
long after all the skating.
The permafrost is destined to harbour gas –
gas that bubbles and dances to music
but cannot open the doors of the houses
or climb into the ovens to cook dinner
for three children. Gas, the only one hungry
because of the permafrost.
Gas destined to burn.

ice

a woman at the window
of a cabin in Norway
ice: an arm around a waist
a white wedding
the reindeer at her window
busking for breakfast blueberries
cloudberries ice: the reindeer's
eyes a groom learning to melt
the reindeer scattering
warm wishes of snow
the best man's speech
words that leave
a woman at the window
the ice more blue there

the sorrows of ice

Letters to Shackleton
(from Henry Worsley)

Isolation

Strange rhythms of ice
soon gripped my mind
whenever I spoke or sang.
My words hid in soft snow,
the silence so cruel
I once convinced myself
        my sledge
was my daughter's coffin
I had to haul
over a rough white field
until she woke.
        From you, Boss,
sometimes a cough
sometimes the arc or shadow
of a storm petrel,
flight feathers from a skua.

Endurance

The wind stuffed one of her sleeves
with my tent, pulled
a bunting of blue petrels
through the other
small holes in the ice.
The coarse tongues of hail
cursed and stoned my sledge.

Some days, sliding one ski
in front of the other was like
threading a needle.

Grytiviken Cemetery

We're ash and bone,
cross and cairn,
nine points of a star.
Huge clouds hang
over us like doors,
the summit just out of reach.
Our custodians,
fur seals, sea elephants,
watch tourists sprinkle
Scotch whisky on our headstones.
Do they think we're still thirsty?
Let's drink to that!
Down at the derelict whaling station
the wind spins the teeth of rotary saws
and turns massive propellers.

Elephant Island to South Georgia

Frank Worsley
(1916)

Tim Jarvis
(2013)

once ice drew the *James Caird*
so low in the water
my navigation tables swam
the huge swell hid
our view of the skyline
South Georgia an albatross
in the wind's feathers
a floating tin eye
when the bow plates opened
I saw the jittery sun

on the *Alexandra Shackleton*
we needed to sleep
below deck in a space
the size of a pantry
all hips and backbone
with wooden wings
we feared a container ship
would surely drown us
I already had trench foot
the compass magnetic dry

What the dogs wrote

breath icicles
hang from my lips
      Nell
slipping on tongues of ice
      a new dance
      Fluffy
how soon my voice
      becomes soft snow
      Lupoid
from Ocean Camp only a glimpse –
      the ship's funnel
      Sailor
we grow hoods of eye fur
      so we can't see
      the g – n
      Unknown

pale pink flames

Under the muslin
of ice, krill
are glinting like mirrors,

like pale pink flames.
They daze algae,
snag floating plants,
light up the ice.

Chains of krill
are spilling into the night,
swimming for their lives.

The sea warmer,
the whoosh of krill smaller.

On watch: Frank Worsley's memorial, Akaroa

I don't need to measure
the sun to know I'm home.
The leaning wooden cottages,
the cormorant, its hooked bill.

Stormy nights, I'm back on watch,
navigating brutal winds, icebergs,
snatching hoosh off the primus.
Any thought of sleeping
is a kind of drowning.
The sound of boots
on a sodden deck.

drift

In his white light dreams
at Discovery Hut,
Herbert Ponting meets
the Siberian ponies
he once photographed
on the *Terra Nova*.

The ponies refuse to wear
equine pyjamas, or bamboo snow shoes
for his Royal Collection.

Inside the stomach of ice,
the ponies soften
the silver shadows
of Scott and his men.
They turn from Herbert's bromide

into the drift
and whiff of themselves

te hau o te atua | the breath of heaven

1

Ōtamahua Quail Island – never used to living alone,
stuck at home behind windows of tarutaru,
fringes of toetoe – watches stables split
and cup in the southerly, watches rust
gnaw sledges, bits and bridles, watches neglect
collapse dog kennels, still finds old stitches
of hoof and paw, tilting her towards the stout
heart of Antarctica.

2

To get to sleep, Rebecca relives walking
around Ōtamahua, past the dog kennels,
to Ivan Skelton's cottage. She goes down
to his grave at South Point, its slim waist
of gritty soil, its Lord's Prayer in a plastic coat,
its lonely white cross . . . over the hill
to the Ship Graveyard, their bones rocking
in loose steel jackets . . . down to where conger eels
rise from the dusky sea and slither up sharp cliffs
through wet feathery grass to wait in
the stagnant pond. Her father . . . *hurry*
Rebecca if you miss this ferry you'll have
to stay on the island.

3

Ponies pull Scott and Shackleton around
Ōtamahua in wheeled sledges. Their iron
harness keeps them in line, helps them steer
the ropes and laws of ice, makes them heroic.
They grow manes of toetoe, hooves of basalt.
They run to Walkers Beach, where fallen pines
puncture the sea, they run to Saddle Gully

through tassels of wind,
and though they leave for Antarctica,
they never leave here.

4
Under the eaves of the leper's hut,
swallows spin the mouth of a nest, trumpets
of swallows low and fearless. All day their cup
fills, their cup empties. Handfuls of swallows
all hush and tremor, swallows as light
as the only leper in their care, Ivan Skelton, confined
by his own skin, hears in his sleep the sea
weaving a path towards his father in Apia,
towards his mother whispering into shells.
He hears now the sudden fierce change
from longing to lament, and lurches awake.
The door is open, the swallows inside,
their shadows a carousel on the rough pine walls,
each swallow each swallow each swallow
raising its wings
like oars
bursting into light
blessing Ivan
just as the tulafale
blows the conch

5
Some afternoons, clouds sweep and baste Ōtamahua
with sun. The island illuminates dog and pony tracks,
Ivan's hut, his grave, the shallows where ships sleep.
Each time Sheryl passes Ōtamahua she remembers
stories of the young farmers Henry and Edward

swept from their boat into Ward's Bay.
In her sleep their eyes find a pathway
through Te Whakaraupō Lyttelton Harbour,
find the waka that will carry them home.

6
The explorers leave Te Whakaraupō.
The slap slap of waves like *sorry* like *sorry* . . .
They sail their wooden rooms into the mouth
of a relentless rolling sea.
The ponies, sliding one ski in front of the other,
travel towards ice that may never release them,
follow the compass from deep waters to white pastures.
Someone here
with frozen breath and muslin hood writes
> *Plant toetoe harakeke tarutaru*
> *to shield Ōtamahua from*
> *shadows / of / ice*

7
Bill's cabin returns tongue-and-groove unused
from Antarctica to Joseph Kinsey's garden.
Te hau o te atua / the breath of heaven.
A chapel for Oriana Wilson, who prays for months
the ice sends the doctor home. A bedroom
for Kathleen Scott, who knows
the doctor and captain lie frozen beneath the Ross Ice Shelf.
A kennel for the husky Osman the Great to remember
the wave that swept him off the *Terra Nova* and the wave
that swept him on again. Bill's cabin now at Godley Head
watching Ōtamahua, hearing in the wind
the sorrows of ice.

Weave a kete
Fill it with
waiata / for / waiting

8
In all weathers the sledge dog stands on the corner
of London and Canterbury streets
looking across to Ōtamahua
waiting for the captain's whistle.
                Hear in the winds
                the song of the anchor
                her / stout / heart

9
At Rāpaki Marae, Te Poho o Tamatea's voice rises
over the rough music of waves,
calling the Antarctic
explorers back to the world of light,
welcoming them to first cast
anchor at Te Rāpaki-o-Te Rakiwhakaputa,
to pray and rest in the strong arms
of Whare Taoka, the carved house.
                Call in the waka
                Let the sisters light
                the spirit pathway
                Ōtamahua / Quail / Island.

Notes

'I've never written to please Ted'
Ted Hughes, the English poet, used to set poetry exercises –
sometimes about a church or a churchyard or an elm tree to
name a few examples. A few years back I stayed in a house in
Eastbourne, England that was right next to an old stone church
and its churchyard. It had a huge elm tree that fell one night
during a violent storm. It set me thinking about Ted Hughes and
this poem was the outcome.

'more horse than castle'
Written after a weekend stay at Larnarch's Castle, Dunedin.

'the trumpet player'
Written for a friend, Michael Gibbs, for many years a trumpet
player with the New Zealand Symphony Orchestra.

'half-mast'
The *Leonardo* was the last of the Island Bay fishing fleet crewed
by the local Italian community. It was made famous by featuring
in the painting by Rita Angus, Boats Island Bay. Part of the
Leonardo's original mast ended up as finials on the roof of my
garden shed!

'if you're looking for Leonard'
The fictional arrival of Leonard Cohen at Tower Hill Tube
Station, London.

'Kalene Hill 1948: the baby won't turn'
'en route to Fish Hoek'
These poems are based on events in the life of my husband, who
was born and lived in Southern Africa as a child.

'instead of travelling north'
This poem was inspired by a picture essay by Dmitry Kokh about polar bears living in an abandoned Arctic weather station.

'blue'
'from letters to Johanna'
Niaqornat is a village in Greenland. Johanna is a fictional character.

'te hau o te atua | the breath of heaven'
Ōtamahua Quail Island is an uninhabited island in Whakaraupō Lyttelton Harbour. It was once home to a leper colony. It has strong links to the Antarctic explorers Scott and Shackleton, who used it as a location to train their huskies for expeditions to the Antarctic.

Acknowledgements

Some of the poems in this book were first published in slightly different forms in other publications. Thank you to the editors of *Acumen, berlin lit, Blackbox Manifold, Geometry, Landfall, London Grip, NZ Poetry Shelf, Pedestal, Poetry* (US), *Poetry NZ, PN Review, Sport, Stand, The Lake Poetry, The Quick Brown Dog, The Unexpected Greenness of Trees* and *Turbine | Kapohau.*

Acknowledgements are also due to the judges of several poetry competitions. My poem 'sure-footed' was highly commended in the 2016 Caselberg Trust International Poetry Competition, 'the ways of rain' was shortlisted in the 2020 Alpine Fellowship Writing Prize and 'blue' was awarded second prize in the inaugural 2020 Acumen International Poetry Competition. The sequence 'te hau o te atua | the breath of heaven' was joint runner-up for the Kathleen Grattan Prize for a Sequence of Poems in 2021.

Thank you to the Michael King Writers' Centre, where I wrote 'the sorrows of ice' during a residency in 2021.

Thank you to Creative New Zealand, who provided an arts continuity grant in 2020.

Thanks and appreciation for their support and encouragement to Bill Manhire, Fergus Barrowman, Spencer Levine, Ashleigh Young, Vincent O'Sullivan, Siobhan Harvey, Stephanie Burt, Jennifer Manson, Frankie McMillan, Marjory Woodfield, Christine Leighton, Rebecca Ball, Helaina Coote and Marisa Cappetta.